ROMAN LONDON

Jenny

HER MAJESTY'S
STATIONERY OFFICE
IN ASSOCIATION WITH
THE MUSEUM OF LONDON

Cover illustrations:

(front) Londinium, looking south-east, during the building of the defensive wall c. AD 200. A detail from the illustration on page 11

(left) Earliest known map of Roman London by William Stukeley, 1722.

Bronze head of the Emperor Hadrian, found in the Thames near London Bridge. Larger than life-size, it possibly commemorated his visit to London in AD 122

CREDITS

The following objects are from the collections of the British Museum (those asterisked have replicas on display in the Museum of London):
Legionary helmet* *figure 8*
Sword and sheath* *9*
Tablet with *procurator*'s stamp *15*
Celsus tombstone* *23*
Gold *solidus* of Magnus
    Maximus* *29*
Smithfield buckle* *36*
Silver ingot* *37*
Bacchus on tiger mosaic *47*
Head of Hadrian* *title page*
Londinio graffito *back cover*

Copyright in the illustrations lies with the Museum of London except for the following:
Londinium looking south-east, *private collection 20*
Inside the Roman fort, *City of London Police 63*
Roman pottery recorded by John Conyers, *The British Library 119*
Museum of Charles Roach Smith, *Guildhall Library, City of London 120*
Basilica drawings by Henry Hodge, *Guildhall Library, City of London 121*

Photographs:
Barrington Gray, John Edwards, Trevor Hurst, Jon Bailey, Jan Scrivener

Illustrations:
Alan and Richard Sorrell
Lyn D Brooks Associates

Design:
David Challis

Filmsetting:
Jolly & Barber Limited

Origination:
Grantown Graphics Limited

© *Crown Copyright 1986*
© *Copyright the Board of Governors of the Museum of London 1986: text and illustrations*
First published 1986

Printed for HMSO by
W S Cowell Limited

DD 737376 C200 8/86

PREFACE

The story of Roman London has developed as the practice of archaeology over the last 300 years has revealed evidence of the Roman settlement. Greatly increased archaeological work within the last ten years in the City and Southwark has resulted in many new discoveries. These important results have been included in order to give a full and up-to-date account of the history of Roman London. *Roman London* has been prepared as a companion to *Londinium: a descriptive map and guide to Roman London* (published by Ordnance Survey). It is also one of the series of books on the history of London produced by the Museum of London.

Jenny Hall
Senior Assistant Keeper in the Prehistoric and Roman Department, Museum of London

Ralph Merrifield
Former Deputy Director and Keeper of the Prehistoric and Roman Department Museum of London

CONTENTS

3 HISTORY OF ROMAN LONDON
4 BEGINNING OF LONDON
8 LONDON AS THE CAPITAL OF ROMAN BRITAIN
14 END OF ROMAN LONDON

17 FABRIC OF ROMAN LONDON
18 BUILDINGS OF ROMAN LONDON
22 ROMAN LONDON'S PORT
25 ROMAN LONDON'S FORT
27 ROMAN LONDON'S WALLS

33 LIFE IN ROMAN LONDON
34 ROMAN LONDONERS
38 LONDON'S TRADE WITH THE EMPIRE
40 RELIGION IN ROMAN LONDON

45 GUIDE TO ROMAN LONDON
46 HISTORY OF DISCOVERY
48 ROMAN LONDON TODAY
48 BOOKLIST
ROMAN OCCUPATION OF BRITAIN AND LONDON *(facing 48)*

HMSO BOOKS

HMSO PUBLICATIONS ARE AVAILABLE FROM:
HMSO BOOKSHOPS
49 High Holborn, London, WC1V 6HB (01) 211 5656 *(Counter service only)*
258 Broad Street, Birmingham, B1 2HE (021) 643 3757
Southey House, 33 Wine Street, Bristol, BS1 2BQ (0272) 24306/24307
9–21 Princess Street, Manchester, M60 8AS (061) 834 7201
80 Chichester Street, Belfast, BT1 4JY (0232) 238451
13a Castle Street, Edinburgh, EH2 3AR (031) 225 6333
HMSO'S ACCREDITED AGENTS *(see Yellow Pages)*
AND THROUGH GOOD BOOKSELLERS

1
Gold medallion from Arras, France,
depicting *Londinium. London welcomes
Constantius Chlorus, who rescued the city
from being plundered* AD *296*

BEGINNING OF LONDON

The story of London as a city began soon after the Roman invasion of AD 43. For centuries before this date the London area seems to have been of great importance as the gateway of Britain, because the Thames provided a highway for water transport into the interior, and this lay immediately opposite an even greater water highway into the heart of Europe – the River Rhine. The western part of what is now Greater London provided land approaches to the river and fords by which it could easily be crossed. Men of the Bronze Age and pre-Roman Iron Age met here for trade and religious ceremonies but, as far as we know, no single riverside settlement of such importance that it could be considered the ancestor of London was ever established – perhaps because the river was then a frontier between tribes who were often at war.

The Roman army from its coastal invasion bases gained control of much of the south east of England and both sides of the River Thames. The most important place in Britain at this time was *Camulodunum* (Colchester) in Essex, which had been the capital of Cunobelinus, a king who had ruled over a large part of south-east England. The Emperor Claudius had decided to make this the capital of the new Roman province, and therefore an overland route crossing the River Thames was needed from the channel ports of Kent into Essex.

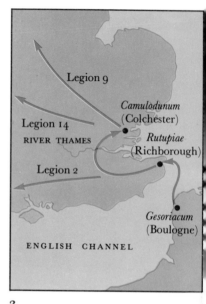

2
The route of the Claudian invasion and initial area of conquest

3 (FAR LEFT)
The Thames formed a boundary between warring tribes

4
The Iron-Age tribes of southern Britain at the time of the Claudian invasion:

1 BRIGANTES
2 PARISI
3 CORITANI
4 DECEANGLI
5 ORDOVICES
6 CORNOVII
7 ICENI
8 TRINOVANTES
9 CATEVALLAUNI
10 DOBUNNI
11 SILURES
12 DEMETAE
13 DUMNONII
14 DUROTRIGES
15 ATREBATES
16 CANTIACI

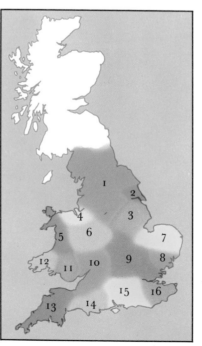

5
Road in Southwark: method of construction used to build over the marshy terrain

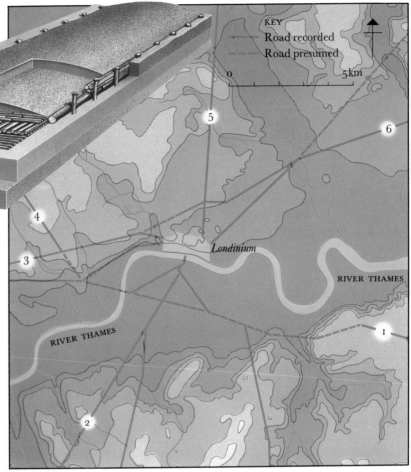

KEY
Road recorded
Road presumed

0   5km

Londinium

RIVER THAMES

RIVER THAMES

6
Roman roads in the London area:
1 WATLING STREET
  To Canterbury (*Durovernum*)
2 STANE STREET
  To Chichester (*Noviomagus*)
3 To Silchester (*Calleva*)
4 WATLING STREET
  To St Albans (*Verulamium*)
5 ERMINE STREET
  To York (*Eburacum*)
6 To Colchester (*Camulodunum*)

7
The late 1st-century quay at its south-western corner (*left*) cutting into the north wall of the possible bridge pier base, the rest of which is covered by modern concrete (*right*). *This base is interpreted as part of the first of London's bridges*

Much remains to be discovered about the position of this first crossing, the nature of the river, and the date of the foundation of the settlement on the north bank of the River Thames in the area now known as the City.

Recent archaeological work in Southwark has discovered two Roman roads which converge on a point just upstream of the medieval bridge (Old London Bridge) and about 20 metres downstream of the present bridge. At the opposite point on the north bank (on the east side of Fish Street Hill), a wooden box-structure adjoining a later Roman quayside has been interpreted as a bridge pier support. The dating evidence for the construction of the Southwark roads and their adjacent occupation however indicates that they may not have been built before AD 50. Since their existence is of primary importance to the establishment of the main settlement on the north bank, it has been suggested that the bridging of the river at this point and the foundation of *Londinium* did not commence until some 7 to 8 years after the initial invasion of AD 43. In addition the known alignment of the arterial Roman road of Watling Street, north and south of the river, on a point in the Westminster–Lambeth area has led to the suggestion that the recorded river crossing and ensuing battle of the invasion force of AD 43 took place to the west of the City.

Whatever the date, the terrain on which the first London developed had a number of natural advantages. On the north bank the gravel terrace with its capping of brickearth rose about 11 to 12 metres above modern Ordnance Datum, and although divided by a small stream (later called the Walbrook), provided a relatively flat platform for building, protected to the west by another larger river (the Fleet) and to the north by the marshy headwaters of the Walbrook. Opposite, on the south bank, the position was less favourable with many intersecting waterways and areas liable to flooding. It was however less marshy than to the east or west, and sand and silt banks gave a marginally higher and drier approach to the river's edge.

The nature of the river must also have influenced the choice of the bridging point. Recent examination of deposits from the Roman fore-shore indicate that in the mid 1st century AD the river was tidal in the City area, though with a minimal rise and fall (about 1.5 metres) and perhaps marking the upstream limit of the tidal head in the Thames estuary at that time.

The resulting choice provided a regular crossing that became a focal point for the developing road system in south-east Britain and at a point on the river that provided deep water for ships within a tidal zone. The construction and material of the first Roman bridge remain uncertain, though a wooden structure may be supposed. Since two Roman sailing-ships have been found upstream of it, they could also pass through it, probably by means of a draw-bridge section that could be raised. London Bridge has since been rebuilt a number of times but has never moved far from the position chosen by the Romans.

Whether in AD 43 or some 7 years later, there can be no doubt that military necessity provided the impetus for the bridging of the Thames and the establishment of a settlement on the north bank. The character of the first occupation is uncertain. Evidence of very early military occupation was found in 1972 near Aldgate, where a v-shaped defensive ditch seems to have been dug and back-filled before the road to *Camulodunum* was constructed. Its fill contained part of the bone grip of a Roman sword. Nearer the bridgehead, clear evidence of military influence is less identifiable, though the laid-out grid structure of the earliest streets may reflect the work of the Roman army.

Both the Roman government and private traders took advantage of the convenience of the site. A flourishing town and port therefore soon grew up at the northern end of the bridge. The Romans called it *Londinium*, a word partly of pre-Roman origin, which may therefore come from the original British name of this place. As no trace has been found of a pre-Roman Iron Age settlement here, it may have been only the name of a farm or its owner.

The first London came to a tragic end when it was destroyed by fire in AD 60. It was one of the towns burnt by Queen Boudica (Boadicea) when she led her tribe, the Iceni of East Anglia, joined by the Trinovantes of Essex, in revolt against the Romans. Suetonius Paulinus, the Governor of Britain, was suppressing the Druids in Anglesey at the time of the revolt. He made an effort to save London, which he actually reached with the Roman cavalry before Boudica's arrival, but decided his force was not strong enough to save the town, and therefore evacuated it with all the inhabitants who were willing and able to leave. Those who did not were massacred, and it may be that some of the skulls found in the Roman stream-bed of the Walbrook were thrown in at this time, perhaps in accordance with some barbaric

8
Roman legionary helmet, mid 1st century AD, from the Thames at London

9
Roman officer's sword, early to mid 1st century AD, from the Thames at Fulham

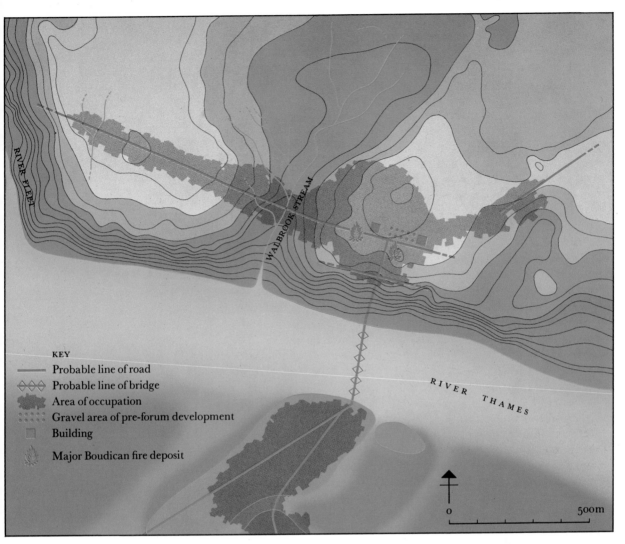

KEY
— Probable line of road
◇◇◇ Probable line of bridge
▓ Area of occupation
░ Gravel area of pre-forum development
□ Building
✿ Major Boudican fire deposit

RIVER FLEET

WALBROOK STREAM

RIVER THAMES

0   500m

10
The early development of *Londinium* and the Roman settlement, south of the River Thames, in Southwark *c*. AD 50–60

11 (LEFT)
Boudican massacre at *Londinium*, AD 60

custom of the tribesmen. A more certain trace of the disaster is a layer of orange-red burnt clay, often observed in excavations in the neighbourhood of Lombard Street and Gracechurch Street, just above the level of the natural ground, now deeply buried under later accumulations. These are the remains of houses with walls of wattle and daub – clay on a frame of timber and withies. The wooden parts have been completely destroyed, and are indicated only by their impressions in the clay, which is burnt to the consistency of terracotta. Underlying the burnt daub is found pottery of the mid 1st century which serves to date the fire. The distribution of this burnt layer shows that the first *Londinium* was mainly on the east side of the Walbrook.

12
Skulls found in the stream-bed of the Walbrook. *Victims of the Boudican massacre?*

London was soon rebuilt, and became the centre of government for the province in all matters connected with finance and economic development. These were under the control of the *procurator*, a high official appointed by the emperor, to whom he was directly responsible. Decianus Catus, the *procurator* whose greed and cruelty had led to the revolt of Boudica, was replaced by Julius Classicianus, a wise and humane official, who disapproved of the severe punishment of the Iceni and Trinovantes that was being carried out by Suetonius Paulinus. He appealed to the Emperor Nero, pointing out that valuable agricultural land was being devastated and its farms destroyed. As a result, an inquiry was held and Suetonius Paulinus was replaced by a new governor. Classicianus evidently had his headquarters in London, where he died a few years later. Part of his tombstone, with an inscription giving his name and title, was found re-used as building material in a bastion (projecting tower) of the city wall on Tower Hill. The inscription is in two pieces. The first portion with part of the ornament from the top of the tomb was found in 1852. This included the name Classicianus, possibly a *procurator* mentioned by Tacitus. The second fragment found in 1935, still *in situ* at the bottom of the bastion, confirmed that the inscription did indeed refer to the *procurator* Classicianus. The monument is now in the British Museum, but a cast of the inscription can be seen in the Museum of London.

Also in the British Museum is a wooden writing-tablet branded with a stamp saying that it was 'issued by the Imperial *Procurators* of the Province of Britain'. It was found in the stream-bed of the Walbrook, and had evidently been used in the *procurator*'s London office. An iron stamp with the letters M P BR was also probably used by one of the *procurator*'s staff in London to mark soft metal such as gold or lead. It is obviously an official stamp, and the initials may stand for METALLA PROVINCIAE BRITANNIAE ('Mines of the Province of Britain'). A government brickworks in London was also probably under the control of the *procurator*. It made bricks and tiles for the public buildings of *Londinium*, and stamped them with the letters P P BR or P PR BR, often with the addition of LON for LONDINII ('at London'). P BR or PR BR stand for PROVINCIAE BRITANNIAE ('of the Province of Britain') and it is possible that the first P stands for the *procurator* himself rather than some lesser official on his staff.

The governor was commander-in-chief of the armies, so he spent much of his time on the frontiers of the province, dealing with whatever trouble was foremost at the time. In the winter, however, he was able to turn his attention to other matters, and it seems likely that he found London the most convenient place in which to do so, because of its accessibility to all parts of the province, as well as to higher authority

13
Tomb of Julius Classicianus, *Procurator* in AD 61. *As procurator, he pressed for leniency for the tribes involved in the Boudican rebellion*

14 (RIGHT)
The public buildings of *Londinium* and the Roman settlement in Southwark *c. AD 100–125. London had expanded rapidly but as yet had no city wall for its defence*

Evidence for the existence of the *procurator*'s office in *Londinium*:

15 (RIGHT)
Wooden writing tablet. *It is branded with the official stamp*

16 (CENTRE)
Iron stamp and enlarged impression. *It was probably used for officially marking metal ingots*

17 (FAR RIGHT)
Building tile. *Its stamp indicates that it was made in the government brickworks, controlled by the procurator*

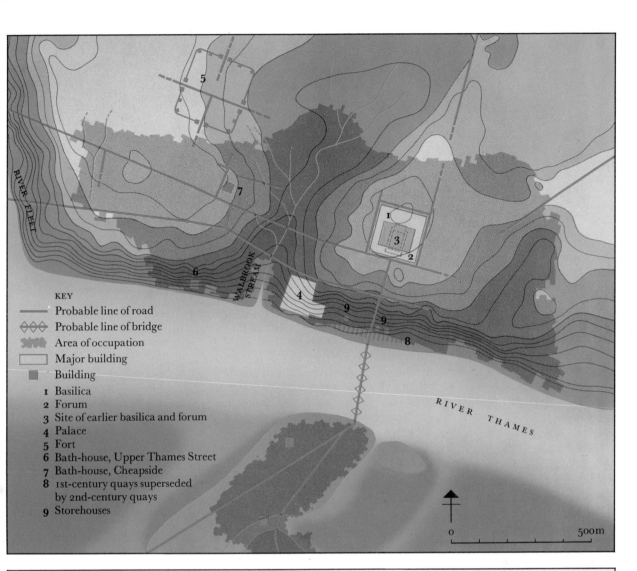

KEY

━━━ Probable line of road

◇◇◇ Probable line of bridge

Area of occupation

▭ Major building

■ Building

1 Basilica
2 Forum
3 Site of earlier basilica and forum
4 Palace
5 Fort
6 Bath-house, Upper Thames Street
7 Bath-house, Cheapside
8 1st-century quays superseded
   by 2nd-century quays
9 Storehouses

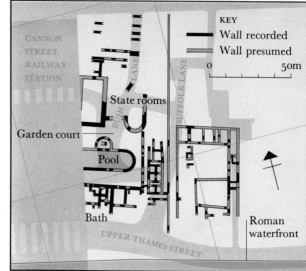

CANNON
STREET
RAILWAY
STATION

State rooms

Garden court

Pool

Bath

Roman
waterfront

UPPER THAMES STREET

KEY
Wall recorded
Wall presumed

0   50m

in Rome. A great building, part of which probably still exists under the arches of Cannon Street Station, was built between AD 80 and 100 on the bank of the Thames near the mouth of the Walbrook. It contained offices and great reception halls as well as living accommodation and extended over an area of at least 13 000 square metres. Although built on a very irregular plan, it was an imposing building with a great ornamental pool in its courtyard. It was clearly an official palace, and it is the only building yet known in Roman London that could have been the governor's winter headquarters.

The symbol of Roman rule in Britain, however, was the great temple to the divinity of the Emperor at *Camulodunum*, at which annual ceremonies were held. The tribes of Britain were responsible for these ceremonies and the upkeep of the temple, and the only body that was representative of the people as a whole had been set up to raise the necessary money and to administer the cult. This was the Provincial Council, to which each tribe had to send representatives.

London was clearly a more convenient centre for the administration of the State cult of Emperor-worship and its transfer from *Camulodunum* may mark London's attainment to the status of capital of the province. The temple at *Camulodunum* had been destroyed by the rebels in AD 60, but for reasons of prestige had to be rebuilt and maintained. Nevertheless, a fragment of an inscription found in Nicholas Lane, and now lost, shows that a temple for Emperor-worship was built in London in the name of the Province of Britain at a fairly early date, and there is also an indication that the headquarters of the Provincial Council were moved to London before AD 100. One of its staff, a slave named Anencletus, buried the ashes of his young wife, Claudia Martina, on Ludgate Hill, where he set up a monument that can be dated to the 1st century by the style of its inscription. It is from scraps of evidence like these that the story of Roman London is reconstructed.

A man who probably knew *Londinium* well was a legionary soldier named Celsus, who was seconded from the Second Legion *Augusta* to serve on the governor's staff as a *speculator*, a kind of military policeman concerned mainly with the execution of justice. He died in London in the 3rd century, and a monument was set up to his memory in the

18 (ABOVE LEFT)
Roman palace, the governor's residence, 2nd century AD

19 (ABOVE)
Plan of the Roman governor's palace, Cannon Street

20 (RIGHT)
Londinium, looking south-east, during the building of the landward wall *c.* AD 200. *The forum and basilica complex (top left) was built on higher ground to the east, separated by the Walbrook stream from the settlement and fort (foreground) in the western area of the city*

21
Bronze seal-box lid, 1st century AD. *It was probably government issue for use with official letters*

24 (RIGHT)
Tombstone of Claudia Martina, from Ludgate Hill. *Her husband was a slave of the Provincial Council*

22 (ABOVE)
Fragment of building inscription. *The building is dedicated to the emperor in the name of the Province of Britain*

23 (RIGHT)
Fragmentary remains of a tombstone of Celsus. *He was seconded to serve on the governor's staff as a military policeman*

Roman coins of the mint of *Londinium* selected to illustrate the mint's history: *The obverse of each coin shows the Emperor's head; the reverse the mint mark. Coins are not reproduced to scale:*

25
Bronze *antoninianus* of Carausius, AD 293. Mint mark ML (*Moneta Londinii*). *The Emperor Carausius established a mint in London in AD 288*

26
Bronze *antoninianus* of Allectus, AD 293–296. Mint mark ML (*Moneta Londinii*). *The London mint continued to produce coins for Carausius' murderer and successor, Allectus*

27
Bronze *follis* of Constantine I as Caesar, AD 307–310. Mint mark PLN (*?Prima (officina) Londinii*). *After the fall of Allectus, the London mint in line with the rest of the Empire adopted the new coinage established by Diocletian*

28
Bronze *follis* of Constantine I, AD 323–324. Mint mark PLON (*?Prima (officina) Londinii*). *Coin minted shortly before the London mint closed down in AD 326*

29
Gold *solidus* of Magnus Maximus, AD 383–388. Mint mark AVG OB (*Augustae obryzum*), 'pure gold of Augusta'. *Augusta was the honorary name for London in the 4th century. The mint was briefly operational again in AD 383–388 under the Emperor Magnus Maximus*

cemetery on Ludgate Hill by his fellow *speculatores*. This inscription in the British Museum is important evidence for the status of *Londinium* in the 3rd century when the province had been reorganised, since *speculatores* were normally based on the capital of a province.

Britain was divided into two separate provinces *c.* AD 200, when York was made the capital of *Britannia Inferior* or Lower Britain, while London remained the capital of *Britannia Superior*, Upper Britain. Another 3rd-century inscription of great importance records the name of a previously unknown provincial governor of Upper Britain. Found re-used as building material in the late Roman riverside wall near Blackfriars, it is the first piece of epigraphic evidence to associate the governorship with *Londinium*. The inscription is on an altar recording that Marcus Martiannius Pulcher *propraetor* (governor or acting-governor) rebuilt a temple of Isis probably some time between AD 251 and 259.

A century later in accordance with the Emperor Diocletian's policy of devolution to improve administrative efficiency, Britain was now further divided into four smaller provinces. London became the capital of *Maxima Caesariensis*, and was also the residence of the *vicarius*, who was a link between the governors of the provinces and higher authority. Throughout, London remained the financial centre for the whole of Britain, and the treasury was still there in the last years of Roman rule. A mint was established in London by the usurping Emperor Carausius in AD 288, and this continued in use after the Empire had resumed proper control of Britain in 296. Its coins were marked with the letters L, LN, or LON for *Londinium*. The mint was closed in 326, but it was started again for a short time by another usurping emperor, Magnus Maximus, in 383, when it used the mint-mark AUG for *Augusta*, a title of honour which had been given to London some years earlier.

30
Altar, 3rd century AD, found re-used in the riverside wall. *It was set up by Marcus Martiannius Pulcher, a provincial governor of Upper Britain whose name was unknown prior to the altar's discovery*

31 (RIGHT)
The province in the 3rd century divided into Lower (*Britannia Inferior*) and Upper Britain (*Britannia Superior*)

32 (FAR RIGHT)
The province in the 4th century divided into four smaller provinces

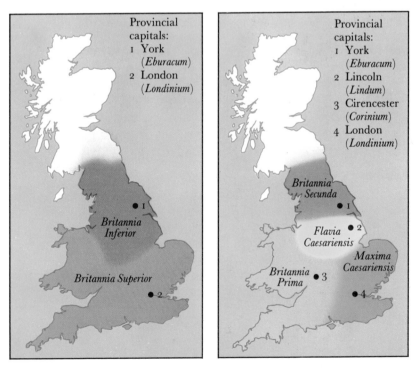

Provincial capitals:
1 York (*Eburacum*)
2 London (*Londinium*)

Britannia Inferior

Britannia Superior

Provincial capitals:
1 York (*Eburacum*)
2 Lincoln (*Lindum*)
3 Cirencester (*Corinium*)
4 London (*Londinium*)

Britannia Secunda

Flavia Caesariensis

Maxima Caesariensis

Britannia Prima

END OF ROMAN LONDON

In AD 410 the Emperor Honorius, in answer to an appeal for help from the local councils of cities in Britain, renounced responsibility for the defence of the province. London, like other walled cities and towns, had to look to its own resources for its defence against the threat of increasing attacks from Saxons and related German tribes across the North Sea. The limited archaeological evidence provides an incomplete picture of the character of the Roman city in these troubled times. The city's defences were maintained and strengthened. Towers had been added to the landward wall in *c.* AD 350 (*see page 30*) and a length of the riverside wall, constructed some 60 to 70 years before, had been rebuilt at the very end of the 4th century (*see page 32*). Two military buckles, one from the Walbrook, the other made in a Germanic style *c.* AD 400 and from the Roman cemetery area in West Smithfield, hint at the presence in London of German mercenaries employed by the Roman army.

The defensive measures no doubt ensured that *Londinium*, renamed *Augusta* probably after AD 368, continued as a centre of administration for one part of the now sub-divided province. On the evidence of an entry in the *Notitia Dignitatum*, a surviving list of military and civilian posts in the Empire, London was the place where the imperial treasury was kept and an officer in charge was stationed in the last decade of the 4th century. A silver ingot of the type presented to soldiers on the emperor's accession, anniversary or birthday, was found while digging within the Tower of London in 1777 with two gold coins of the Emperors Honorius and Arcadius, who came to the throne in AD 383 and AD 395 respectively.

For the last half of the 4th century the general nature of the occupation within the walls is uncertain. Finds of coins dating to after AD 365 are not numerous, but some twenty find-spots are recorded, the majority being on the east side of the Walbrook. Deposits of 'dark earth' recorded in excavations as smothering the dismantled remains of Roman buildings in the western half of the city suggests that some areas had not been built on since the late 2nd to early 3rd century, and had been put to other uses, perhaps cultivation. There is however a possibility of erosion of late Roman structures by the process that created the 'dark earth'. The full extent of these changes is not clear, though a contraction of the population seems likely.

The best glimpse of the end of Roman London was obtained in an excavation in 1969–70 in Lower Thames Street. Here a large house with under-floor heating, and with its own private bath-suite continued in use into the 5th century. More than two hundred copper coins, of the last imperial issues to reach Britain in quantity, were found scattered on the floor of the furnace-room. They were issued between AD 388 and

33
Coin of the Emperor Honorius. *In AD 410 he renounced responsibility for the defence of British cities*

34 (RIGHT)
Londinium and the Roman settlement in Southwark in the 4th century AD. *Limited archaeological evidence makes the general nature of occupation within the walled area uncertain*

Evidence for the later history of *Londinium*:

35 (RIGHT)
Amphora, 5th century AD, imported from the Eastern Mediterranean. *Nearer sources of supply from Spain and Italy may have been disrupted by barbarian invasions*

36 (CENTRE)
Bronze buckle *c.* AD 400, probably made in the Rhineland. *It was worn by a government official or a regular or mercenary army officer*

37 (FAR RIGHT)
Silver ingot, late 4th century AD, found in 1777 at the Tower of London. *Ingots were presented to soldiers on special imperial occasions*

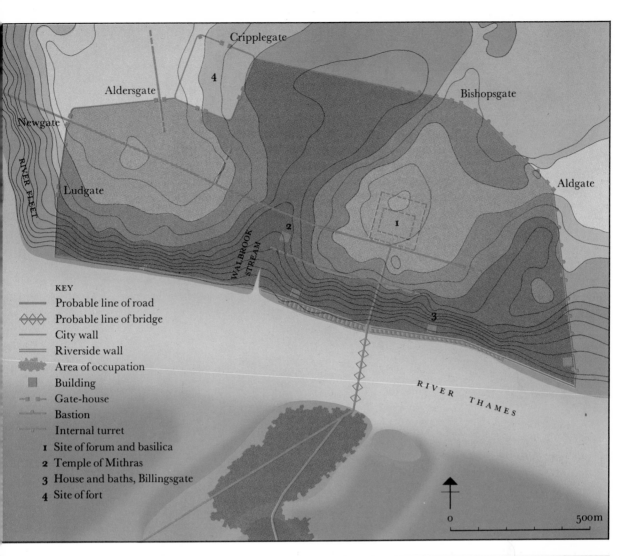

KEY

	Probable line of road
◇◇◇	Probable line of bridge
	City wall
	Riverside wall
	Area of occupation
▪	Building
	Gate-house
	Bastion
	Internal turret
1	Site of forum and basilica
2	Temple of Mithras
3	House and baths, Billingsgate
4	Site of fort

0   500m

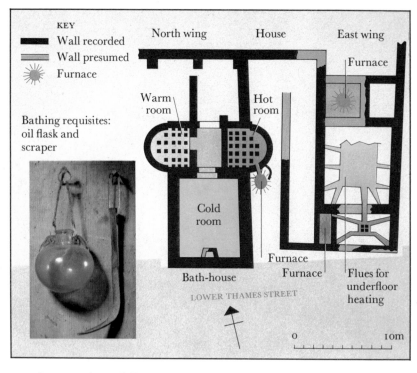

KEY
- ■ Wall recorded
- ▬ Wall presumed
- ☀ Furnace

North wing · House · East wing

Warm room

Hot room

Furnace

Cold room

Bath-house

Furnace · Furnace

Flues for underfloor heating

LOWER THAMES STREET

Bathing requisites: oil flask and scraper

0 ————— 10m

38 (ABOVE)
Private baths: excavation of one of two heated rooms. *Use of the baths had ceased before the house's inhabitants finally left*

39 (LEFT)
Plan of late Roman house and baths, Lower Thames Street

40 (BELOW)
Collapsed roof tiles from the east wing of the late Roman house. *The house was deserted and left to become derelict*

402, but may have fallen on the floor long after that period. Beneath the uncleared ash of the last firing of the furnace, from which hot air passed beneath the floor of the living-quarters, was found a piece of *amphora*. This came from the Eastern Mediterranean, probably from Gaza, and it is likely to be of 5th-century date. It presumably contained wine or some other standard Mediterranean product, and the fact that this was being imported from the farther end of the Roman world suggests that nearer sources of supply had already been disrupted by the barbarian invasions of Spain and Italy in the early 5th century. There is therefore a strong indication that people were still living in London in Roman style, in such houses as this with under-floor heating, after 410 when the Emperor Honorius finally disclaimed responsibility for its defence. Moreover, they were still able to import luxuries, and this must imply that there were exports of some kind to pay for them. The return cargo is likely to have been provided by the troubled nature of the times, and it may be conjectured that, after the collapse of the Western Empire, there was a brief revival in London's fortunes as a centre for trading slaves with the eastern Mediterranean.

The end, however, was soon to come, for this house at least, and it seems to have been by quiet desertion rather than violent destruction. The windows were broken, and the glass fell on the floor. The winds then gradually destroyed the roof, the tiles of which also fell on the floor. At this stage the roofless shell of the bath-house had a visitor, who lost her brooch amongst the roof debris. This is a circular brooch that is almost identical with one from a pagan Saxon grave at Mitcham, Surrey. It is unlikely to be later than mid 5th century in date, so that it would seem that the building was roofless in the third quarter of the century, if not a little earlier. Its walls did not fall down, however, but seem to have been deliberately demolished, after which there is no indication of further occupation or activity on the site for centuries.

41
Late Roman brooch (*above*) identical to early Saxon brooch (*right*). *It is thought that these brooches originated from the same work-shop in Surrey*

42
Mosaic floor from Bucklersbury. *The chromolithograph of 1870 shows the mosaic as recorded. The restored mosaic now forms a central feature in the Roman Gallery at the Museum of London*

BUILDINGS OF ROMAN LONDON

The importance of London was ensured by its geographical advantages. It stands on a tidal river which has always provided easy access to ships. Sea-going ships could travel from the heart of Europe by means of the River Rhine, directly across the North Sea to the Thames estuary. It provided a convenient means of entry into the heart of lowland Britain.

In the 1st century AD the level of the River Thames in the City area was perhaps as much as 4 metres below its present high-water level. The exact width of the river in the Roman period is unknown. It was probably wider and shallower, but would nevertheless have been navigable by Roman sea-going ships.

The physical geography of the region strongly influenced the origin and early development of London. The north bank of the Thames was elevated and well-drained, the south bank low lying and marshy. Where the Rivers Fleet and Walbrook cut into the north terrace, they left two flat-topped promontories of high ground, consisting of gravel capped by yellowish-brown brickearth. These were the initial points of settlement with a constant supply of water from the Walbrook and the River Thames. There were also springs at the base of the gravel which could be exploited by shallow wells. The steep bank of the river was ideal for habitation. Excavations have found that sites have been terraced due to the steepness of the slopes.

Roman towns were classified according to their functions and importance, and given varying constitutions for local government. The highest was a *colonia*, a settlement of Roman citizens with full legal rights, and the second a *municipium*, which could have been a native town whose citizens had more limited rights of franchise. At the time of the Boudican revolt, *Camulodunum* was a *colonia* and *Verulamium* (St Albans) a *municipium*, but all we know of the status of *Londinium* is that it was not then a *colonia*. It seems likely that its status had not yet been defined.

Excavations have shown that the centre of *Londinium* underwent a complicated development in the 1st century AD. In the AD 70s at the time the settlement was rapidly expanding, a substantial public building, probably an early *basilica*, with adjoining rectangular enclosure (*forum*) was built on top of the high ground to the east of the Walbrook. Before the end of the 1st century, however, the centre of *Londinium* was replanned and this earlier development replaced by a great *basilica*, with a *forum* to the south. The *basilica* served as town hall and court of justice, and it was there that the local senate – the City's first Council of Aldermen – would have met. *Londinium* must now have had a constitution for local government, and it would be surprising if it had not been made a *colonia* – especially as it had been provided with a

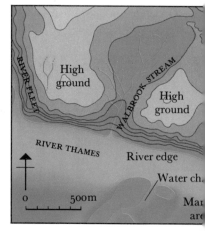

43
The topography of *Londinium* and the Roman settlement in Southwark in the Roman period

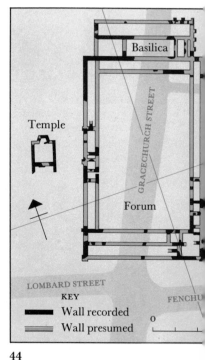

44
Plan of the early *forum* and *basilica*, Gracechurch Street

FABRIC OF ROMAN LONDON

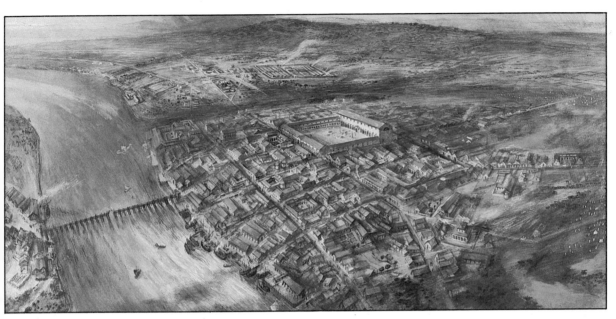

45
Londinium in the reign of Hadrian, *c.* AD 125, from the south-east. *The forum and basilica predominate*

46 (BELOW)
Plan of the second *forum* and *basilica*, built over the earlier complex

47 (BELOW RIGHT)
Mosaic floor with Bacchus on a tiger, from Leadenhall Street

basilica more than 150 metres long, longer than that of any other city north of the Alps. It was a great hall with a nave and northern aisle, adjoining which was a double row of offices. At the eastern end was the tribune, a raised platform for the judges. The eastern portion underlies Leadenhall Market, and the western runs through the site of St Peter's Church and right across Cornhill. The *forum* formed an enclosure on three sides, with the *basilica* on the fourth, around a great central courtyard. Its three wings contained shops and offices, forming the business centre of the city.

Other public buildings, constructed in the late 1st and enlarged in the 2nd century, were bath-houses in Upper Thames Street and Cheapside. Tacitus tells us that his father-in-law, Agricola, when Governor of

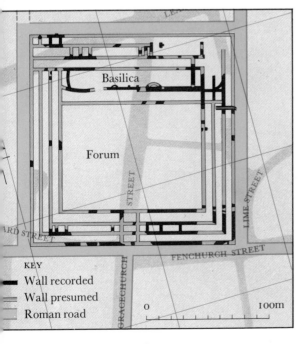

48 (LEFT)
Public baths at
Cheapside.
*Built on a scale
similar to military
bath-houses, it
was positioned
near the fort and
was perhaps for
military use*

49 (ABOVE)
Public baths, Upper Thames Street:
excavation of a large heated room.
*The bricks supported a floor for the
hypocaust heating*

Britain from AD 77–83, encouraged the Britons to adopt the pleasures
of civilisation, including the daily bath. The building of these baths
was no doubt part of this policy. The Cheapside baths were smaller
and similar in scale to military bath-houses while those in Upper
Thames Street were built on a grander scale on the river bank over-
looking the Thames and in a position where natural spring water fed
the baths. They were like a modern Turkish bath, with hot and warm
rooms heated by hot air drawn under the floors and through flues in
the walls. The bather took with him a *strigil* for scraping off the
perspiration and a flask of oil for anointing himself. In later Roman
times it became fashionable for wealthy men to have their own private
bath-houses, and one of these was found in Lower Thames Street (*see
page 16*).

Public buildings and the more substantial private houses were built
of Kentish ragstone and flat tile-like bricks, at least for the lower parts
of their walls. The ragstone was often used with lime mortar to make a
very hard rubble concrete. Floors were sometimes made of *opus signinum*,
a sort of concrete that contained fragments of broken tile. The better
floors, however, were mosaics of small cubes of variously coloured
stone, making patterns and pictures. Roofs were often of flanged tiles
(*tegulae*) overlaid by curved tiles (*imbrices*), of the kind still used in
Mediterranean countries. Many of the poorer houses and shops, however, and sometimes parts of the better buildings, were made of wood,
with walls of wattle and daub, often covered with painted plaster, and
with thatched roofs. There must have been danger of fire, and most of
the city was in fact burnt for the second time, probably this time
accidentally, *c*.125–130.

Recent excavations of domestic buildings at three sites west of the
Walbrook have provided evidence of the recovery of this area after the
fire, and its subsequent development. In Milk Street, a building with
a fine mosaic pavement was soon erected but by the end of the
2nd century this was abandoned and there is little trace of later
Roman occupation. In Newgate Street, buildings were destroyed by
the fire and there followed an extensive planned redevelopment of the
area. Two substantial timber-framed commercial premises were built.
They were connected at the first floor to cover an alley running
between them. Shops fronted on to the street, with storage and small-
scale production facilities in small rooms behind. These shops had been
dismantled by AD 200 with no clear evidence of any successors.

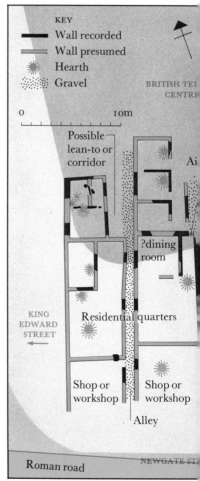

KEY
▬ Wall recorded
▬ Wall presumed
✳ Hearth
⣿ Gravel

50
Plan of late 1st-century buildings,
Newgate Street. *The buildings were for
commercial use*

51
Excavation of a 2nd-century mosaic decorated with a *cantharus*, Milk Street. *The mosaic formed the floor of a substantial timber building*

52 (BELOW)
Construction techniques for buildings in *Londinium*

of tiles: *tegula*   *imbrex*

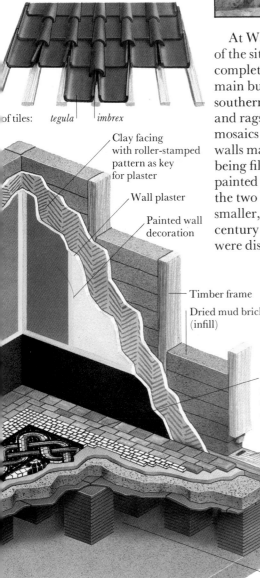

Clay facing with roller-stamped pattern as key for plaster

Wall plaster

Painted wall decoration

Timber frame

Dried mud brick (infill)

Decorated mosaic floor set in mortar

Timber base plate

Soil

Underfloor heating system

At Watling Court, to the south of Cheapside, a major development of the site had taken place before AD 100, providing one of the most complete areas of domestic building recovered from the City. Three main buildings, each of a different construction, filled the site. The southern building was timber-framed but stood on low walls of flint and ragstone. It had a corridor leading to rooms which contained mosaics and *opus signinum* floors. The northern structure in part had walls made of courses of broken roof tiles, the timber-frame above being filled with unfired mud bricks. The walls were covered with painted wall-plaster and traces of mosaic were found. The area between the two buildings, originally open, had been eventually filled in with a smaller, poorer structure. This complex, too, was destroyed in the 2nd-century fire. Buildings of a poor quality replaced them but they too were disused by AD 200.

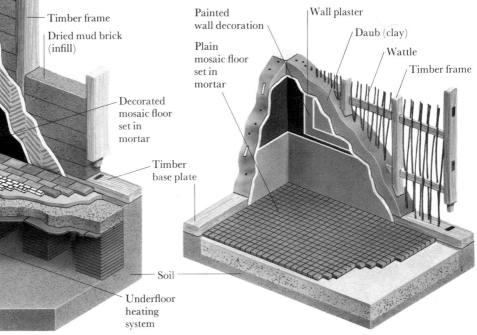

Painted wall decoration

Plain mosaic floor set in mortar

Wall plaster

Daub (clay)

Wattle

Timber frame

ROMAN LONDON'S PORT

The commercial vitality and subsequent growth that characterised the Roman city after AD 60, depended on the construction of adequate port facilities along the river's edge. From recent excavations we now have a clearer picture of these waterfronts, their operation and their continual development.

The river bank in the mid 1st century AD lay to the north of modern Lower and Upper Thames Street. The building and replacement of successive waterfronts throughout the Roman, medieval and later periods, has resulted in today's river edge lying some 100 metres or more further to the south.

Three main constructional phases in the Roman era have been identified, although it remains uncertain whether these represent the building of a waterfront along a substantial length of the river bank at the direction of the city's authorities, or individual quays developed on the initiative of *negotiatores*, wholesale import-export merchants.

53
Waterfront storehouses: reconstructed from evidence at Pudding Lane

Excavations near Pudding Lane, adjacent to and immediately downstream of the Roman bridge, revealed a wooden landing stage of mid 1st-century date. It had been dismantled and replaced some 20 years later by a major timber-faced quay. The front of the quay was constructed of squared timber baulks (0.6×0.4 metres in section) laid horizontally on top of each other and braced behind with timber tiebacks. This framework had been infilled with dumped deposits of earth and debris, creating a level platform for the unloading of goods and their removal into the two rectangular transit storehouses found a few metres to the north. These buildings, measuring 25×6 metres, were each subdivided into five equal bays and were stone-built with wooden planked floors, wide doors and an upper storey. Although separated from the quayside as it was rebuilt further south, the buildings continued in use until at least the end of the 4th century AD. It is clear from similar discoveries at Miles Lane that the same facilities for shipping had also been developed upstream of the bridge by the late 1st century.

These waterfronts were superseded when a new one was built in the 2nd century AD out into the river (now under Thames Street), and the land reclaimed between the two. This quay was in turn replaced by a major waterfront development in the early part of the 3rd century AD, which has been located and examined in three places south of the modern street, at Custom House west of the Tower of London, by St Magnus church just downstream of the Roman bridge, and upstream at Seal House. At the first site, massive timbers laid horizontally again formed the front with a multiple-box framework of jointed beams behind. Similar if lighter construction was found at the other sites. In total length this 3rd-century waterfront extended for at least

54
Unused pottery (samian), found in the Thames at New Fresh Wharf

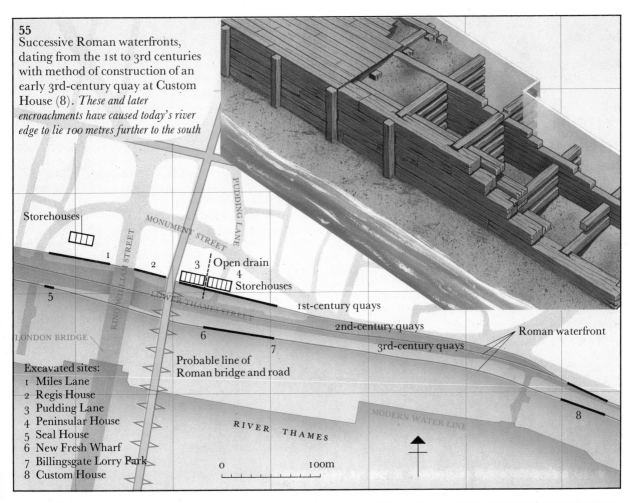

55
Successive Roman waterfronts, dating from the 1st to 3rd centuries with method of construction of an early 3rd-century quay at Custom House (8). *These and later encroachments have caused today's river edge to lie 100 metres further to the south*

Storehouses

MONUMENT STREET

PUDDING LANE

KING WILLIAM STREET

LOWER THAMES STREET

LONDON BRIDGE

1

2

3 Open drain

4 Storehouses

5

6

7

8

1st-century quays

2nd-century quays

3rd-century quays

Roman waterfront

Probable line of Roman bridge and road

MODERN WATER LINE

RIVER THAMES

Excavated sites:
1 Miles Lane
2 Regis House
3 Pudding Lane
4 Peninsular House
5 Seal House
6 New Fresh Wharf
7 Billingsgate Lorry Park
8 Custom House

0   100m

56 (LEFT)
Section of the excavated 1st-century quay at Pudding Lane, looking north. A later 2nd-century open drain cuts through the quay. Behind, storehouses with timber floors opened onto the waterfront

57 (ABOVE)
Reconstruction of 1st-century storehouses and quay. The open drain was later constructed between the existing buildings

550 metres, and represented major construction work, requiring the felling of a great number of trees and the employment of a considerable team of skilled carpenters supported by many more labourers.

Several sailing vessels have been found that had sunk and been buried in the silts of the River Thames. The remains of a flat-bottomed Roman sailing barge with some of its cargo of ragstone still on board, were found near Blackfriars Bridge in 1962. It had probably been built early in the 2nd century (as was indicated by a worn coin of AD 88–9 placed for luck in the mast-step before the mast was set up, in accordance with a custom that still survives). On pottery evidence it had broken up on the river-bed during the 3rd century. This suggests a date for the wreck near the time of building the city wall, and the barge may well have been bringing stone for that purpose. Its capacity was probably about 25 cubic metres, and at least 1300 similar barge-loads would have been needed. Another vessel, a Mediterranean style of merchant ship with round hull and projecting keel, was uncovered at Lambeth in 1910 on the site of County Hall. It dates to the 3rd century.

58 (ABOVE LEFT)
Boat with cargo of ragstone at the entrance to the River Fleet. *The remains of such a boat were found in the Thames at Blackfriars*

59 (ABOVE)
A flat-bottomed Roman sailing barge. *Model of the type found at Blackfriars*

60
Coin of Fortuna, found in the mast-step of the Blackfriars boat. *The coin was placed in position before the mast was stepped, as a symbol of good luck*

61 (LEFT)
Mediterranean style of merchant ship. *Model of the type found at County Hall*

62
Tombstone of legionary soldier. *He was probably attached to the headquarters' staff in a clerical capacity*

3 (BELOW)
nside the Roman fort, looking northast, after the construction of the andward wall. *The fort was primarily sed as barracks for those soldiers working n the governor's staff*

The extent of the debris of the second fire, dated by the burnt pottery found in it, shows that by the early 2nd century *Londinium* had spread well to the west of the Walbrook and also more to the east. The northern part of the city seems to have escaped, and it was here, to the north west of the town, that a fort had recently been built. Its purpose was probably not so much to defend London from attack, as to provide a suitable barracks for troops who were necessarily stationed in the capital city – soldiers for guard duties, escorts and ceremonial, like those in London today. Since Britain was ruled by a military government, it may also have been a home for soldiers like Celsus, who had public duties that today would be carried out by civilians. We do not yet know the exact date when the fort was built, but it may have been one of the improvements made as a result of the visit of the Emperor Hadrian in AD 122, or in anticipation of it. Hadrian would certainly have disapproved of the billeting of soldiers among civilians, and the fort was carefully placed outside the town as it then existed, and well away from the main centre of population.

It covered an area of nearly 5 hectares (12 acres) and was built to the standard pattern – rectangular with rounded corners which contained corner towers. There were also intermediate towers, which presumably contained stairways to a rampart walk. The walls were built of Kentish ragstone, consisting of facings of squared blocks laid in regular courses and a rubble-concrete core. A bank was piled against

the inner face, and an external v-shaped ditch was dug. There were four gates, one in each side, and the lower part of the northern half of the west gate has been preserved under the double carriageway of London Wall (*for opening times, see page 48*). Parts of the fort wall, with foundations of an intermediate turret, and the turret at the south-west corner can be seen to the west of Noble Street. The northern part of modern Wood Street corresponds roughly with the central road through the fort.

A stone figure, originally from a tomb, but re-used in the fill of a bastion in Camomile Street, gives a good idea of the appearance of one of the soldiers of Roman London. He wears a tunic and cloak, with a short sword and studded strap hanging from his belt. His left hand holds a case of wooden writing tablets perhaps indicating that his duties were partly clerical. He is a legionary soldier and probably a junior officer (*optio*), but his presence in London suggests that he was attached to the headquarters' staff. Another tombstone of a Roman soldier, also presumably working at headquarters, depicts a centurion, Vivius Marcianus. He wears a tunic with a military belt and a long cloak. He holds a centurion's staff in his right hand and perhaps a scroll in his left. Auxiliary soldiers (who, unlike legionaries, were not Roman citizens) were no doubt also stationed in London to serve as guards and escorts, and one is represented with the distinctive oval shield of an auxiliary on a tombstone, presumably found in the City. Weapons found in London include spearheads of the kind used by auxiliary guards, and possibly by legionaries for ceremonial purposes, swordgrips and daggers. One fine example of an iron dagger and scabbard is likely to have been part of the equipment of an auxiliary soldier. The cumbersome javelins used by legionaries in the field have not been found in *Londinium*. There are, however, arrowheads and *ballista* bolts, as well as notched bone plates from composite bows.

64
Tombstone of a Roman centurion Vivius Marcianus, found in Ludgate Hill 1669. *He holds a centurion's staff and scroll*

65 (BELOW)
Iron dagger and scabbard, from Copthall Court. *They are likely to have belonged to an auxiliary soldier*

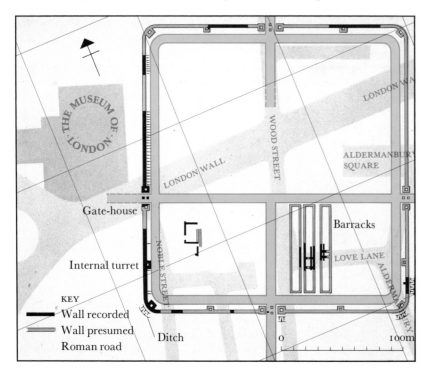

KEY
Wall recorded
Wall presumed
Roman road

Gate-house
Internal turret
Ditch

THE MUSEUM OF LONDON
LONDON WALL
WOOD STREET
LONDON WALL
NOBLE STREET
ALDERMANBURY SQUARE
Barracks
LOVE LANE
ALDERMANBURY

o   100m

66 (LEFT)
Plan of the Roman fort, built early 2nd century AD

FABRIC OF ROMAN LONDO

7
A surviving section of City wall at
Tower Hill. *This section of wall still
stands to a height of 10.6 metres, of which
the lower section is Roman*

In *c.* AD 200 a decision was taken that was to determine the shape of
London for the next 1300 years, and has left its mark on the City to this
day. This was the enclosure of the whole of *Londinium* with a great wall –
a tremendous task, for which there must have been an impelling
reason. It may have been a safety measure to protect the capital during
the civil war at the end of the 2nd century, when Clodius Albinus,
Governor of Britain, tried to make himself emperor, and took most of
the troops in Britain to fight his battles on the Continent. We have
known for some time that the wall was not built earlier than *c.* AD 190
on the evidence of a coin of AD 183–4 and a great deal of pottery found
in deposits earlier than its construction. For evidence that it is not likely
to have been built later than *c.*210, we are indebted to a forger, who
was busily making imitation silver coins (*denarii*) in London *c.* AD 200.
For this purpose he made terracotta moulds from genuine unworn
coins of AD 201–10, 210–12 and 215. Perhaps surprised in his work and
wishing to dispose of the evidence, he threw away the moulds, together
with a genuine new *denarius* of 213–17 and several earlier bronze coins,
under the stairway of a tower in the city wall in Old Bailey, where
quite a lot of rubbish had already accumulated since the building of
the wall.

The wall extended round the east, north and west sides of the
Roman city, from the site of the Tower of London to Blackfriars, a
distance of more than 3 kilometres. It was 2.7 metres thick at ground

8
The walled circuit of *Londinium*
, AD 200. *The uniform construction
of such a long wall was a considerable
engineering task*

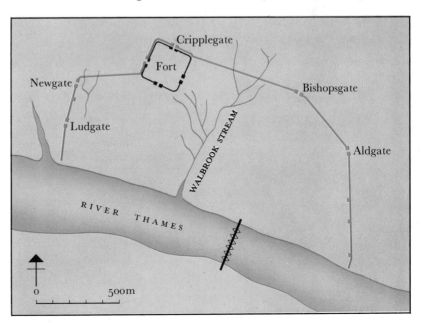

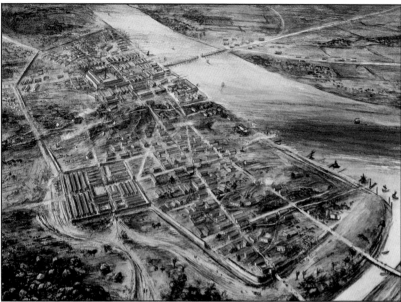

69

Aerial view of *Londinium* from the north-west, showing sections of the defensive wall during its constructio *c.* AD 200. *The wall stretched from the River Thames, forming a northern bounda to the town, and incorporated existing buildings, including the fort (left foreground)*

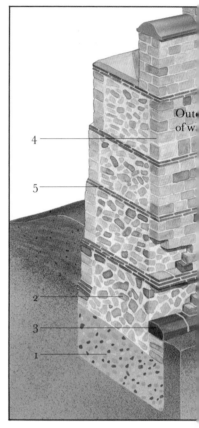

level, where it was faced on the outside with a sandstone plinth, and just over 2.4 metres thick above this. We do not know the original height, but it has survived in recent times to a height of 4.4 metres, and was probably at least 6 metres high when built. The main material was ragstone, quarried in the Maidstone district of Kent, and at least 86 000 tonnes of this would have been required. It was brought down the River Medway and up the Thames by water.

The faces of the walls were built of squared blocks of ragstone, shaped by masons so that they could be laid in regular courses like bricks. More than a million of these would have been needed – a considerable task requiring skilled labour. When the two faces had been built up to a height of about a metre, the space between was filled

Evidence for the construction of the landward wall at 6–7 The Crescent:

70 (FAR LEFT)
View of the outer face of the wall revealing the foundations and sandstone plinth (*bottom*); squared blocks of ragstone and tile courses (*centre*) an rubble infill (*top, centre*)

71 (LEFT)
View of the wall. This recently-excavated Roman section of wall survives to a height of 2.45 metres. *The accumulation against the wall (righ here shown in section, is the result of the nearly 1800 years of continuous occupatio which has buried Roman London*

with irregular lumps of ragstone, around which mortar was poured. Two or three courses of tiles were then laid over the top for stability, and on this platform the same process was repeated. This went on until the wall was of the required height, so that the courses of tiles run horizontally through it at regular intervals.

There is only one part of the wall in which they are not found. This is where two sides of the earlier fort have been incorporated in the city wall. Here two perfectly sound walls were already standing, and both labour and material could be saved by using them. The line of the city wall was therefore laid so that it joined the north-east and south-west corners of the fort, and the north and west walls of the fort became in effect part of the new wall. They were, however, less than half the thickness intended for the city wall, so a second wall was built as a thickening along the inside of the two fort walls to bring this part of the city defences up to the standard strength. In St Alphege garden the double Roman wall from the north side of the fort can be seen with medieval rebuilding above, but here the outer (fort) wall has been much reduced in thickness and re-faced at an early date. It can be seen better on the west side of the fort both to the north of the gate preserved under London Wall and on the west side of Noble Street.

The approach to the wall on the outside was defended by a ditch about 4 metres from the face of the wall. The earth dug from this and from the foundation trench was eventually piled up against the inner face of the wall to form a great bank, which added to its strength.

Where the Roman roads left *Londinium* at Aldgate, Bishopsgate, Newgate and Ludgate, gate-houses were built. If the fort continued in existence after the wall was built, as is quite likely, then the north and west gates of the fort also became Roman city gates, although their use by the general public was presumably restricted. The north gate, Cripplegate, never led to an important road, but remained in use. Excavations, however, show that the west gate was blocked up before the medieval period. Aldersgate seems to have been added as a later Roman insertion, after the wall was built, perhaps as a replacement for the west gate in a more convenient position. A late-medieval gate was inserted at Moorgate, but otherwise later gates remained on the same sites as the original Roman gates until all gates were finally demolished in the 18th century to improve traffic access.

The wall fell into decay during the Saxon period and large sections of the Roman wall were repaired or rebuilt in the 12th to 17th centuries

on the same line, except in the south-west corner where it was extended to the River Fleet in the 13th century. After the 17th century, as London expanded rapidly in size, the wall was no longer necessary for defence. During the 18th century most of it had disappeared. Only recently have several sections again become visible. Other portions survive in private basements and underground carparks. Good portions of the Roman wall can be seen on Tower Hill and in Cooper's Row. In both cases, the Roman wall survives to just above modern ground level. The Roman sections (4.4 metres) stand to the height of the sentry walk. There is medieval stonework above.

75
Stone lion, found in a tower in Camomile Street. *It had been re-used as building material and probably came from the nearby cemetery at Bishopsgate*

76 (LEFT)
A newly-constructed 4th-century bastion. *One of a series built on the eastern side of Roman London in the 4th century*

Bastions – semi-circular projecting towers – were eventually built on to the outside of the city wall. With one exception, those in the western part of the city are hollow from the base; some, and probably all, of these are medieval. Most of those on the eastern side, however, are solid, and contain re-used Roman building material, including fragments of monuments and tombstones from the neighbouring Roman cemeteries. At least twenty towers were added to the eastern side of the city wall in the troubled years of the later 4th century. One just north of Aldgate, excavated in 1971, and built prior to the formation of a layer of rubble that contained coins and pottery of the later 4th century, suggests a construction date of *c*. AD 350. These towers were probably 8 to 9 metres high and were built to strengthen the defences and provide platforms for *ballistae* (catapults). Their outer curving walls were built from ragstone like the wall itself, but lacked the regular tile courses. Since three hitherto unknown bastions have been found in recent years and a convincing case has been argued for five more, it is very likely that they were spaced at regular intervals of about 60 metres along the eastern defences. At Emperor House, Vine Street, the chalk foundations for the base of one of these towers can be seen. Many of the towers were re-used in the medieval and later defences but this tower had been demolished by the 13th century.

For nearly a century after the wall on the landward side was built, it was considered an adequate defence for *Londinium*. The river alone must have been thought to be a suitable barrier to the south, although excavations in 1974 revealed the foundations of a tower, 8 metres

77
City wall and chalk foundations of la Roman tower, during excavations in Vine Street. *The towers, built from ragstone, also contained monumental stone fragments stripped from nearby cemeteries*

The additional defences of *Londinium*, built in the later 3rd and 4th centuries AD. *The riverside wall and bastions, on the eastern side of the city, were added to protect the city from attackers sailing up-river*

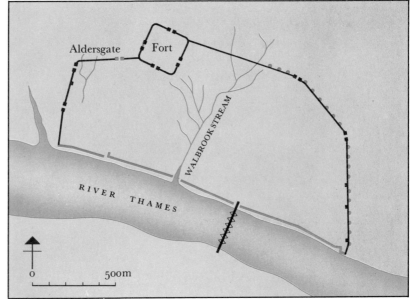

KEY
— Line of city wall
— Line of riverside wall
◇◇◇ Probable line of bridge
▪▪▪ Gate-house
▪▪▪ Bastion
▪▪▪ Internal turret

Evidence for the irregular construction of one section of the riverside wall re-using monumental stone:

79 (ABOVE)
Sculptured block depicting the god Mars and purse and shoulder of Mercury. *Sculptures of deities originated from a monumental arch and screen*

80
Monumental arch: reconstruction model in the Roman Gallery of the Museum of London. *The arch presumably stood in a religious precinct near to where this stretch of the riverside wall was built in the south-west corner of the city*

square, built in the late 3rd century at Shadwell, 1.2 kilometres to the east of the city. It is thought to be perhaps one of a series of signal towers to keep watch on the river. In addition, however, in the late 3rd and 4th centuries, the east and west ends of the landward wall were joined by a new wall that ran along the river-front north of the wharves, approximately on the line of Upper and Lower Thames Street.

Evidence for this wall was found as early as 1841 but theories varied as to its purpose and date. Sufficient sections have been found in recent years to show that it was a continuous defensive wall. In 1974–5 excavations uncovered a massive collapsed length of the wall at Blackfriars. It was found that there were two styles of wall construction. In the eastern part there was a 40-metre length of wall built of ragstone with tile courses constructed in a similar (but less precise) manner to the landward wall. Its foundation was of rows of oak-piles rammed into the underlying gravel, with a thick layer of chalk above. Reconsideration of the dating evidence from the oak-piles has suggested the late 3rd century for the construction here. In the western part of the site, the riverside wall had no elaborate foundation, simply large ragstone blocks rammed into the clay. It had token tile courses on the inner face only and it contained stone blocks re-used from a demolished monumental arch and screen of late 2nd to 3rd-century date, and mid 3rd-century inscriptions. The re-used stone suggests that it may have been built hurriedly in a time of crisis at a later date some time in the 4th century.

In 1977 and 1978, excavations within the Tower of London exposed the eastern end of the wall just inside the Inner Curtain wall of the Tower. Here the original wall had been either rebuilt later, further to the north, or a secondary wall had been built while the original wall was still standing. The later wall however did not continue in a straight line to the east, as did the original wall in order to meet the landward wall, but turned south at an angle. The reason for building such a defensive promontory is unclear. This later wall had slight foundations of clay mixed with flint, ragstone and chalk, and was faced on its northern side with neatly-squared blocks of stone. The outer face consisted of ragstone with one double course of tiles. Abundant coin evidence from below a clay bank supporting the rear of the wall indicated that it had been built at the very end of the 4th century.

The lack of consistency in the construction of the riverside wall by comparison with the earlier landward wall, suggests that it may not all have been built at the same time. However, it is known that it was gradually destroyed by river action, which undermined its foundations, and by the 10th and 11th centuries it had collapsed.

81
Oak-pile foundations for riverside wall, Upper Thames Street. *For some stretches of the riverside wall the nature of the ground dictated the use of piles to provide an adequate foundation*

82
The collapsed riverside wall with re-used sculptured blocks *in situ. The foundations of the riverside wall were gradually eroded by the river and the wall had collapsed inwards by the 10th and 11th centuries*

83 (LEFT)
Riverside wall, at its south-eastern corner, Tower of London. The brick Inner Curtain wall of the Tower (*left*) cuts into the outer face. A viewing platform has been constructed (*right*). *Rebuilt further north in the late 4th century, this section formed a defensive corner at its junction with the landward wall*

LIFE IN ROMAN LONDON

The busy waterfront at *Londinium*
c. AD 100: reconstruction model in the
Museum of London, based on recent
archaeological excavations. *The*
commercial vitality and rapid growth of
Roman London after AD 60 *depended on the*
port facilities. The imports that passed
through improved the quality of life. The
port and its associated trades provided
livelihoods for many of London's inhabitants
and meant prosperity for London's growing
population

ROMAN LONDONERS

Londinium was a cosmopolitan city and its inhabitants were a mixed people. Many were of British or Gaulish origin; others came from far-reaching parts of the Empire. There were Roman citizens, the free who were not citizens, those freed from slavery, and slaves. Many of the Roman citizens that we know of from London came as administrators of the province or as soldiers. Romans of Italian origin must have formed only a small part of this official class, in which Roman citizens of Gaulish descent, like Classicianus, were more numerous. In due course, native-born Britons would have aspired to positions in the provincial administration, so that the upper class of *Londinium*, though politically and culturally Roman, must have been a constantly changing racial mixture.

Below the official establishment were the merchants and financiers of differing nationalities. Some were Roman citizens, such as Aulus Alfidius Olussa, born in Athens, whose tombstone is in the British Museum. Others, such as Rufus of Celtic origin, whose letter concerning his London business interests has survived, were not citizens, but were evidently men of substance. The native-born free and those freed from slavery probably formed the bulk of the population, as local craftsmen, shopkeepers and labourers. Even the slaves, probably mostly Britons, could rise to positions of some importance and responsibility, as did Anencletus, a slave of the Provincial Council (*see page 10*). Most slaves in London would have been employed as servants, craftsmen and clerks.

Tacitus tells us Agricola was so successful in civilising the Britons that the *toga* was to be seen everywhere. A tombstone shows the kind of civilian dress that might have been worn on formal occasions by the citizens of *Londinium*. The main figure wears a form of voluminous drapery – either a *toga*, a semi-circular garment that was the formal dress of a Roman citizen, or a *pallium*, a rectangular cloak of Greek

85
Tombstone showing a man wearing a *toga* and a small boy wearing a tunic and cape

86 (LEFT)
Lady's dressing table: reconstruction in the Museum of London. *The brooches, pins and bracelets are often found on Roman sites. All the artefacts here were found in London*

87 (LEFT)
Head of a bone hair-pin. *It represents a lady with an elaborate hairstyle of the late 1st century* AD

88 (BELOW)
Statue of a child with ball, 2nd century AD, found in Westminster. *Perhaps a funerary portrait, the statue depicts a child, four to five years old, wearing a cloak and holding a ball*

89 (BELOW)
Leather bikini trunks from 1st-century well, Queen Street. *They may have belonged to a young acrobatic dancer*

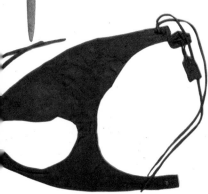

origin. Either would have been most inconvenient in the muddy streets of *Londinium*. On ordinary occasions a costume like that of the small boy would have been worn. He wears a tunic and a short cape, fastened on each shoulder with a bronze brooch. Usually the cape had a hood which was pulled over the head in bad weather.

Brooches, such as those used to fasten tunics and cloaks, formed a part of the personal ornaments and toilet accessories that everyone used. Ladies' hair-pins of bronze and bone are particularly common and a fine example in bone shows why so many were required. It represents the head of a young lady, with a hair-style fashionable in the late 1st century. Ladies' hair-styles changed as frequently as they do now, but were always based on long hair, so that hair-pins were usually required.

The only examples of actual dress to survive from *Londinium* are those made of leather, which remains in good condition when water-logged. Boot-soles with hobnails and various kinds of sandal, mostly moccasin-style fastened by lacing, are found in the Walbrook stream-bed and as rubbish thrown down Roman wells. The most interesting Roman leather articles from London, however, are two pairs of 'bikini' trunks. Both pairs are very brief and could only have been worn by a young girl, who may have been an acrobatic dancer. They were fastened by means of long laces, tied at the hips. One pair are without decoration, the others are decorated with openwork and are frilled around the legs.

Field sports were no doubt popular – hunting in the forests around *Londinium*, where deer and wild boar were to be found. Pottery cups and beakers decorated with hunt scenes were common and spearheads and wild boar tusks from Roman sites in London may be relics of the sport. There was fishing in the Thames and its tributaries, as shown by the bronze fish-hooks found.

Children's games were very similar to those of today, with ball games, hoops and tops probably being used. A small statue from West-minster depicts a child holding a ball. Board games were played with dice carved from bone and jet, and counters made of bone, decorated glass and pottery, all of which have been found in Roman levels in London.

Latin was in general use in Roman London, at least as a written language. The many examples of graffiti scratched on walls, tiles, pots and writing tablets suggest that some knowledge of reading and writing was widespread. A sentence in bad Latin written on the soft clay of a newly-made building tile tells us not only that 'Austalis has been wandering off on his own every day for a fortnight', but that Latin was in everyday use in brickyards. A stone stamp, with an inscription in reverse on its four sides, records four different medical preparations for various eye troubles. One side reads 'Caius Silvius Tetricus' salve for an attack of inflammation'. The stone was probably used to stamp sticks of ointment by impressing them with one of the inscribed sides.

Inked inscriptions are sometimes found on *amphorae*, great earthen-ware jars, either recording the quantity or revealing the contents of the container. From this and from the archaeological evidence it is possible to study the food and diet of Roman Londoners. Most of the animal bone remains that are excavated represent the discarded refuse from slaughter yards and houses. Beef was the meat most frequently eaten,

Stone stamp recording four different medical preparations for eye troubles. *It was used by the oculist for marking packets of eye ointment*

91 (ABOVE)
Building tile with scratched inscription. *It complains about a worker's absenteeism from the brickworks*

then pork. Very little mutton seems to have been consumed. Their meat diet was supplemented by such game animals as red and roe deer. Oysters were a favourite common dish, the shells being found in profusion on many excavated sites. The fish bones that have been studied show that such fish as ling and cod were eaten. The most common birds for the table appear to have been domestic chicken, goose and duck.

The Roman cook used a wide selection of herbs similar to those in modern cookery. They used dill, coriander and fennel as spices. Fruits which may have been grown locally included apples, pears, quince, cherries and plums. Olives and dried figs were imported. Their pips and stones have survived. Seeds from vegetables survive less well. In London, however, there is evidence for cucumbers and peas. Lentils and walnuts were also eaten.

To satisfy the needs of a large urban community which demanded more than the bare necessities of life, a variety of service-trades and crafts were required. Much of the food of *Londinium* must have come from the surrounding countryside, which also supplied most of the coarse pottery used in its preparation and storage. Jars and bowls of various kinds were made in Highgate Wood, and kitchen vessels including mixing bowls (*mortaria*) at Brockley Hill, between London and St Albans. Some pottery was also made in *Londinium* itself.

Few traces have survived of the numerous merchants in provisions of various kinds, apart from the balances and steelyards which were probably used for weighing-out foodstuffs in their shops and stalls.

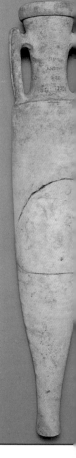

92
Roman *amphora* from Southwark. *It bears an inscription that 'Lucius Tettius Africanus supplies the finest fish sauce from Antipolis (Antibes)'*

93 (LEFT)
Roman kitchen: reconstruction forming a central feature in the Roman Gallery at the Museum of London

94

Pottery for the Romano-British consumer in *Londinium. It was produced locally at Highgate, North London, and Brockley Hill, near St Albans*

95
(BELOW)

Donkey mill: showing method of operation, used for bulk flour production. *Part of such a mill was found near the Bank of England. Large bakers' ovens have also been found in the city and bread was a major item in the diet*

Bread was clearly a major item in the diet of Roman Londoners. A great hour glass-shaped millstone, of the kind used by bakers in Pompeii and Ostia, and turned by horse or donkey, was found near the Bank of England – and other large flat millstones recovered from the stream-bed of the Walbrook suggest that water-driven mills operated within the city. Ovens belonging to a baker's establishment similar to that in Pompeii were built *c.* AD 70–80 but were presumably demolished when the eastern part of the great *forum* was laid out, *c.* AD 90–100.

The tools of carpenters, leatherworkers, smiths, masons and plasterers, remarkably like those of modern times, have been found in considerable numbers in the stream-bed of the Walbrook. There is, however, no indication that these trades were being practised in the immediate area. Builders and stone-masons left behind their picks, trowels, points, dividers and a lewising-tool, used for making mortices in a block of stone for the attachment of a clamp by which it could be hoisted. Plasterers left their small tools; carpenters their chisels, draw-knives, bits, scribing awls, drills and folding foot-rules.

The craftsmen who made these tools stamped their names on their goods. Aprilis and Titulus are two such tool-makers and Basilius, a cutler, is recorded several times. Metalworking in iron, bronze and tin seems to have been important. Before the building of the palace, in Cannon Street, a goldsmith was at work there, for fragments of pottery crucibles bearing traces of gold were found on the site.

96
(RIGHT)

Cutler's stall: reconstruction in the Museum of London. *Craftsmen stamped their names on their tools. One cutler was called Basilius*

97
(FAR RIGHT)

Carpenter's bench: reconstruction in the Museum of London. *The tools of carpenters have been found in the Walbrook stream-bed. They are remarkably like those of modern times*

Trade flourished in *Londinium*, where a prosperous community demanded goods on a par with those being used throughout the Empire. Fine pottery of glossy red ware (samian) was imported in great quantities from Gaul, its place of manufacture. These bowls and plates were made in moulds and were mass-produced on an industrial scale. They were plain or decorated with floral designs, representations of classical myths, hunting scenes or gladitorial combats. Other pottery came from Gaul and the Rhineland. Fine glass was brought from Italy, the Rhineland and the East. Wine was brought in *amphorae* from Italy and Spain, and in wooden barrels from Gaul. From Spain also came olive oil for cooking and lamp fuel, and the fish sauce (*garum*) that was an essential ingredient in most Roman recipes. Other *amphorae* of varying shapes were imported from other parts of the Mediterranean, transporting commodities of various kinds.

In addition, amber in the form of beads came from the Baltic and enamelled bronze brooches came from Belgium. Italy sent fine bronze tableware and pottery lamps. Millstones were transported from Germany and small pipe-clay figures from Gaul. Marble for building and tombstones was quarried in Turkey, Greece, Italy and France.

While the province was developing such imports were essential, since there were no native craftsmen to produce the high quality goods required. As the province grew, its inhabitants became more self-sufficient in such goods as pottery and tableware. Indeed, goods of British origin also flooded into London. Pottery came from nearby Brockley Hill and Highgate for everyday use; beakers with decorative hunting-scenes were made in the Nene Valley, near Peterborough; flagons with decoration in black slip from Alice Holt Forest near Farnham, Surrey, and decorated bowls from Oxford. Lead was brought from Derbyshire and from the Mendip Hills, Somerset, and tin came from Cornwall. The two metals were combined to produce pewter from which items of tableware were manufactured. Beads, rings, hairpins and bangles were made of jet from Whitby, Yorkshire, and bangles, trays and furniture of shale from Kimmeridge in Dorset. Slaves, either to be kept in Britain or traded to the Continent, were taken from amongst the natives living beyond the Roman frontiers.

98
Emerald and gold necklace from Cannon Street. *The emeralds came from Egypt*

99 (ABOVE RIGHT)
Dining room, *c*. AD 100: reconstruction in the Museum of London. *The tableware, bronze jugs and glassware are import*

100 (FAR RIGHT)
Dining room, *c*. AD 300: reconstruction in the Museum of London. *Imports were no longer essential when home-produced items were readily available*

101 (RIGHT)
Imports into *Londinium* from the Roman Empire

102 (BELOW)
British goods brought into *Londinium*

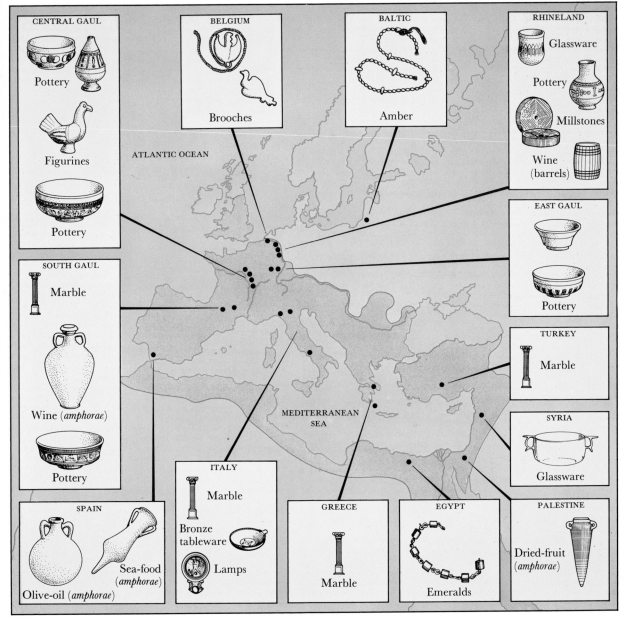

Religion in Roman Britain was a mixture of native Celtic and imported ideas. Roman gods such as Mars and Mercury were worshipped side by side with Celtic deities such as the three mother-goddesses. The Romans for the most part had a business-like attitude towards their gods. Gifts were offered to them in return for favours requested or granted, or to placate them if the worshipper felt he had offended the deity. Their offerings varied according to the size of the request and how much they could afford to pay. It might have been the dedication of an altar, the sacrifice of an animal or bird, or the presentation of a small object. A figure of the god or goddess to whom the request was being made, a model of a part of the body healed by the god, a personal ornament, a coin, or even some object of practical use was considered an appropriate gift.

Religious objects, including certain types of pottery apparently used in religious cults have been found in *Londinium*, mainly in the cemeteries and in the neighbourhood of the Walbrook stream. There are indications that the Walbrook valley became a religious quarter and small shrines probably stood on its banks. This would certainly not have prevented the stream's use for commerce, however, but may even have encouraged it. Amulets of various kinds have been found, as well as votive clay figurines imported from Central Gaul or the Rhineland. The commonest type of figurine, representing Venus after bathing, is a classical subject that elsewhere in Gaul and Britain is associated with sacred springs, and which may also be connected with the cult of a Celtic water-goddess.

Mother-goddess figurines have also been found in the Walbrook valley, as well as a votive tin plaque of the three Celtic mother-goddesses, represented as a trinity. An inscription on a marble plinth from Budge Row evidently came from a shrine of the mother-goddesses that stood nearby, beside the Walbrook. It tells us that 'the district restored (the shrine) in honour of the Mothers at its own expense'. Another temple of the mother-goddesses probably stood somewhere in the eastern part of the city, for a large stone group of the goddesses, unfortunately with their heads missing, was found on a Roman floor near St Olave's Church in Hart Street. Each goddess has a basket of fruit on her lap.

During the excavation of the riverside wall another sculpture, probably from a shrine, was found. This time four mother-goddesses are depicted. Two are holding fruit; one has a dog on her lap, but it is not clear why the fourth female figure nursing a baby has been added. She could be intended to represent not merely a nursing mother-goddess (*Dea Nutrix*) whose cult was common in Gaul, but also a deified empress.

103
Religious plaque of three mother-goddesses.
The worship of mother-goddesses was popular in Roman London

104
Venus figurine made in central Gaul or the Rhineland. *It was a religious offering given as payment to the deity in return for the fulfilment of a vow*

105

Sculpture depicting four mother-goddesses, found later re-used in the riverside wall. *It is not clear why a fourth female figure is represented*

106

Statue of British hunter-god, found in Southwark. *The number of representations of this god from London indicate his popularity*

107

Flagon with inscription, found in Southwark. *It would have been a religious offering at a temple of the goddess Isis*

A possible rival in popularity to the mother-goddesses may have been that of the hunter-god. A fine example from Southwark is believed to be a mixture of a British hunter-god, Apollo and an eastern saviour-god. He holds a bow, with a quiver on his back, and is accompanied by a dog and possibly a stag. Two other figures from the City are perhaps part of the same cult.

The worship of gods and goddesses from Asia and Egypt, such as those of Cybele, the Asiatic great mother-goddess, or the Egyptian goddess, Isis, was introduced to the west under the Roman Empire. These mystery cults were organised as secret societies to which admission was by initiation, and all promised the initiates a happy life after death. There is evidence for the cult of Isis in London in two inscriptions. One inscription is on a wine flagon from Southwark. The flagon, inscribed LONDINI AD FANVM ISIDIS 'At London, at the Temple of Isis', was presumably a votive offering at a temple of Isis, somewhere nearby. The other inscription is to be found on a limestone altar, found re-used in the riverside wall, which commemorates the rebuilding of a temple, probably of Isis (*see page 13*).

The only temple of a mystery cult that has yet been positively identified in London, however, stood on the east bank of the Walbrook, on the site of Bucklersbury House, and was excavated by W F Grimes in 1954. This was a basilican temple, built *c*. AD 240, and architecturally very much like an early Christian church, with central nave and side aisles, divided from the nave on each side by a row of seven columns that supported the roof. At the western end, within a rounded apse, buttressed outside, was a raised sanctuary. The earliest Christian churches also had their sanctuaries at the western end, so that it at first seemed possible that the building might be a church of the Roman period. As the excavation proceeded, however, a group of fine marble sculptures of pagan deities were found. They included a head of Mithras, and from this and other finds it became clear that this was in fact a *Mithraeum*, the worshipping-place of the cult that was Christianity's strongest rival in the Roman world.

Mithras was originally the Persian (or rather Indo-European) god of heavenly light, and his worship came to the Romans by way of Asia Minor, where he acquired the Phrygian cap he always wears. It was only one among many mystery religions introduced from the East. Mithraism was exceptional in that it insisted on a high moral code, with emphasis on honesty, purity and courage. It was especially favoured by soldiers, officials and merchants.

Near the head of Mithras were found the heads of Minerva (without her helmet) and Serapis, Egyptian god of the Underworld, represented with a corn measure on his head, a small figure of Mercury, and a giant hand gripping the hilt of a dagger. All are of Carrara marble and were probably carved in Italy. The hand is that of Mithras, who was most commonly represented in the act of sacrificing a bull, as in a marble relief found in Walbrook in 1889, almost certainly from the *Mithraeum*, together with marble figures of a genius and a river-god, perhaps symbolising London and the Thames. The sacrifice is that of the primeval bull, from which, in Mithraic legend, came the useful life of the earth. The head of Mithras probably came from a similar group, most of which may have been of less precious material, such as stucco; but it is unlikely that the hand ever formed part of a group, which would have been several times life-size.

The sculptures found in 1889 and 1954 were probably buried at the same time. Those found in 1954 were buried in a floor that seems to have been in use early in the 4th century. Since they were deliberately and carefully laid where they were found, it has been suggested that they were buried to save them from desecration by the Christians. Attacks of this kind were common when Christianity gained the ascendancy over its great rival, but they generally occurred considerably later in the 4th century.

The building continued in use, however, and there is no evidence at all that it ever became a Christian church. In its final phase, indeed, another pagan marble sculpture stood in the temple, and was found lying on its latest floor. This is a group representing Bacchus, the wine-god, with Silenus, a satyr, a maenad, a panther and a serpent. The

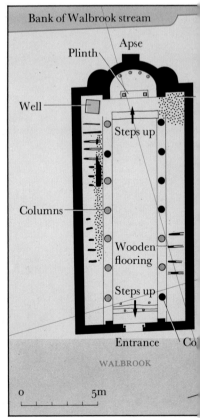

108 (LEFT)
Marble head of Mithras, the god of heavenly light. *Mithraism was one of the mystery religions introduced from the East*

109 (BOTTOM LEFT)
Interior of the Temple of Mithras. *Mystery religions acted as secret societies with initiation rites known only to members*

110 (LOWER LEFT)
Plan of the Temple of Mithras. *The base of the temple has been reconstructed in Queen Victoria Street, using the original building material*

111 (FAR RIGHT)
Silver box and strainer. *It may have been associated with an initiation ceremony*

112 (RIGHT)
Head of Serapis, Egyptian god of the Underworld. *One of a group of pagan deities found during excavations in 1954. The sculptures were buried to protect them from desecration by Christians*

113 (LOWER RIGHT)
Sculpture, depicting Bacchus with Silenus, a satyr, maenad and panther. *This sculpture was found on the latest floor of the temple when the building was no longer used to worship Mithras*

114 (BELOW)
Sacrificial scene depicting Mithras slaying the bull. *Found in Walbrook in 1889, it certainly formed a major sculpture in the worship of Mithras and undoubtedly came from the temple*

Latin inscription, '(Give) life to wandering men', suggests that the wine-god was here regarded as a saviour.

Perhaps the most mysterious find in the *Mithraeum* was a unique silver box, containing a strainer or infuser. It was found after the removal of a 19th-century foundation that had been cut into the north wall, and must have been in a secret hiding-place in the wall itself. Its purpose is uncertain, and the symbolism of the figures of men and animals on the box is obscure. It may be connected with the idea of death and re-birth associated with an initiation ceremony.

Thoughts of life after death were certainly in the minds of the worshippers in the *Mithraeum* where Serapis, lord of the dead, and Mercury (Hermes), guide of departed spirits on their last journey, were prominent among the gods represented. Belief in an after-life is also shown by the finds associated with burials, where food, drink, lamps and personal possessions were buried with the dead for their journey to the next world. Most of the perfect pottery and glass vessels in the Museum of London were found in the Roman cemeteries, where

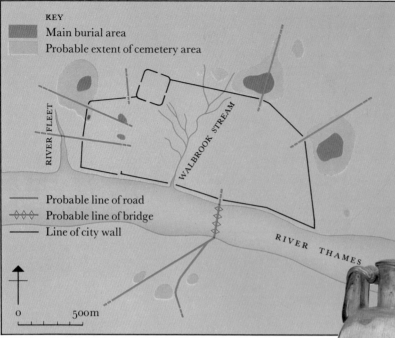

KEY

Main burial area

Probable extent of cemetery area

RIVER FLEET

WALBROOK STREAM

RIVER THAMES

— Probable line of road
◇◇◇ Probable line of bridge
— Line of city wall

0   500m

The cemetery areas of *Londinium* and the Roman settlement in Southwark. *It was Roman practice to place the cemeterie[s] outside the town, along the main roads*

Burial group from Roman cemetery area, Bishopsgate. *Cremation was the usual practice until the late 2nd century. The large vessel contains the cremated bone[s]*

they had been placed in graves, either as urns for the ashes of the dead, or as containers of food and drink. By Roman law the dead had to be buried outside the city limits. In *Londinium* the cemeteries were mostly beyond the city wall. Some earlier burials occur inside the wall when the city limits were smaller.

Cremation was the general rule in Britain until the 3rd century, when there was a gradual change to the practice of burying the unburnt body. There are however several early inhumations and late cremations in London. The great increase in popularity of burying the body was not entirely due to the spread of Christian ideas of the resurrection of the body, for many of these burials are pagan. Bodies were interred either directly in the ground, sometimes with a lining of gypsum for embalming purposes, or in wooden, stone or marble coffins. A 4th-century coffin of imported marble found containing a skeleton in Lower Clapton, Hackney, has the figure of a woman in relief upon it.

By the 3rd century Christianity had spread throughout the Empire. There is very little archaeological evidence of Christianity in *Londinium*, but, like other Roman towns, it must have been predominantly Christian through most of the 4th century. In 312 the Emperor Constantine was converted to Christianity and the religion became officially recognised. Two years later a Bishop of *Londinium*, named Restitutus, attended the Council of Arles, suggesting that there must have been Christian churches or at least a Christian community in the city by this date.

The only surviving evidence is a small pewter bowl with a 'Chi-Rho' symbol (the first two Greek letters of the name of Christ) scratched on the base, and several late Roman pewter ingots found in the Thames near Battersea Bridge, stamped with the Chi-Rho monogram and the words SPES IN DEO ('Hope in God'). There is also an old tradition that St Peter-upon-Cornhill was founded in Roman times but there is no real evidence that any existing City church is of Roman origin.

Christian monogram on base of pewter bowl, from Copthall Court. *The 'Chi-Rho' symbol denotes the first two Greek letters of the name of Christ*

GUIDE TO ROMAN LONDON

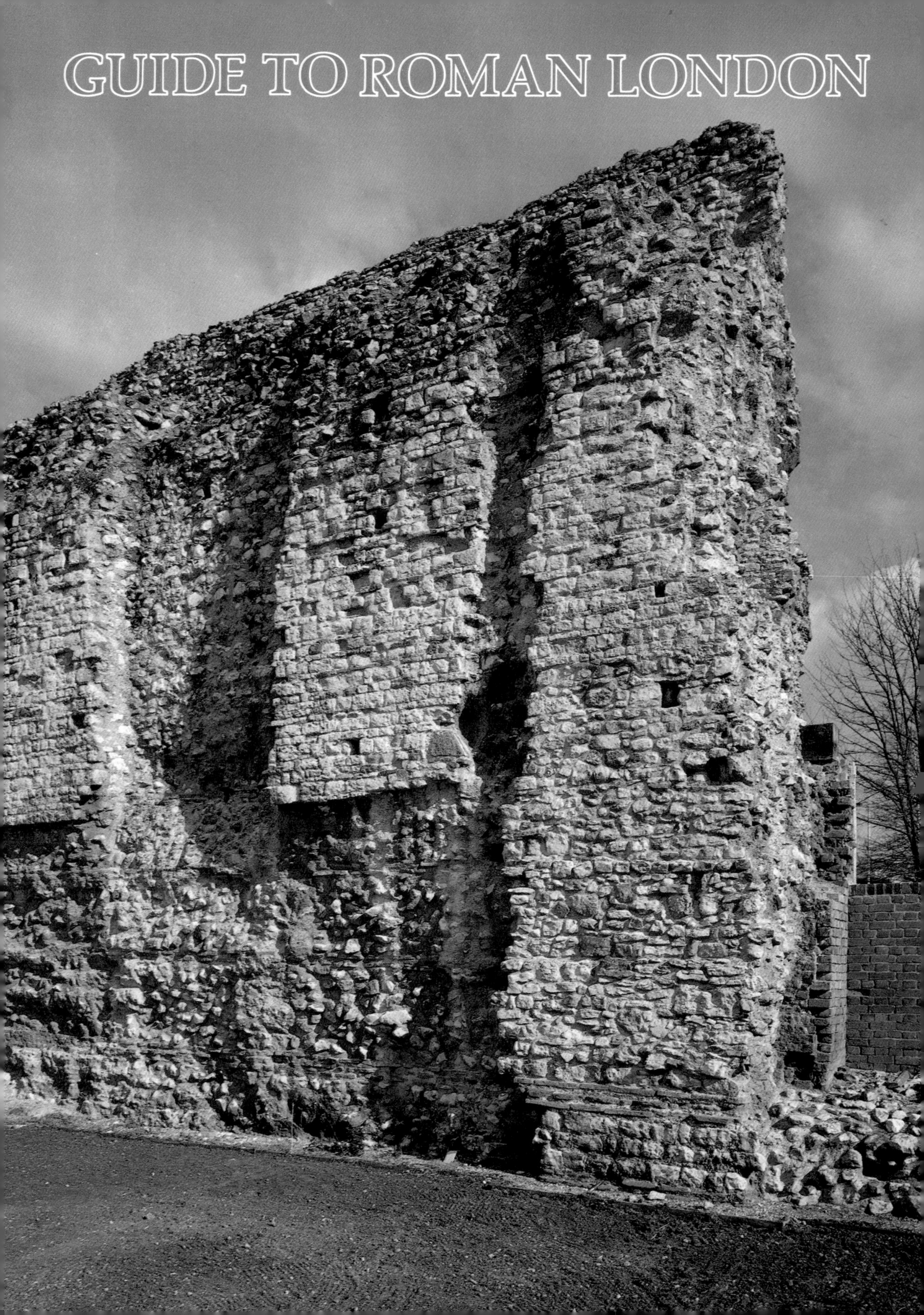

Our knowledge today of the history and archaeology of Roman London has resulted from countless discoveries and observations from below the streets and pavements of the City over the last 200 years.

Although the Tudor historian John Stow in his *Survey of London*, published in 1598, included some archaeological observations, particularly of what he saw of a Roman cemetery being unearthed at Spitalfields, it was the extensive rebuilding of London after the Great Fire of 1666 that gave the first real opportunity for archaeological investigations.

This reconstruction of large parts of the City took place at a time of great scientific investigation and discovery, stimulating enquiry into the origins of civilisation as well as examination of the surrounding natural world. Several learned men became interested in the origins of London and formed collections from the many antiquities being unearthed in the building operations. The 17th-century antiquarians included Sir Christopher Wren, John Conyers, a pharmacist living at the foot of Ludgate Hill, who drew Roman kilns and pottery found during the rebuilding of St Paul's Cathedral, and Dr John Woodward, who acquired much of Conyers' large collection, and in 1713 published a tract on his archaeological observations at Bishopsgate and his thoughts on the history of the ancient city.

1722 saw the first published plan of the Roman city, drawn by the great antiquary and topographical recorder, William Stukeley, though the detailed layout of the city and its features owe more to the draughtsman's imagination than recorded archaeological observations. Again, it was the physical disturbance of the City, this time in the 19th century with the dramatic increase in new buildings for offices, the laying out of new streets and road-widening schemes and the construction of sewers and underground railways, that resulted in the opportunity for many new discoveries. These included not only the collection of objects, but also the recording of mosaics, fragments of Roman buildings, and lengths of the walled defences. In the early part of the century Charles Roach Smith was the City's most indefatigable archaeologist, collecting, recording and publishing Roman and medieval material with great zeal. On his retirement from City life in 1855, the contents of his private museum passed by purchase to the British Museum.

Official response to this increased public awareness and interest in archaeology resulted in the opening of the Guildhall Museum by the Corporation of London in 1876. The Bucklersbury mosaic discovered in 1869 outside the Mansion House during the construction of the new thoroughfare, Queen Victoria Street, was one of the major exhibits. Also displayed were the fragments of Roman sculpture found re-used in the Roman bastions on the city wall, carefully saved and recorded

118 (PAGE 45)
Roman and medieval wall at Tower Hill. *It still stands to a height of 10.6 metres. The Roman work survives to the level of the sentry walk (4.4 metres) with medieval stonework above*

119
Roman pottery as recorded by John Conyers in 1677. *He recorded Roman kilns and pottery found during the rebuilding of St Paul's Cathedral after the Great Fire*

The museum of Charles Roach Smith at NO.5 Liverpool Street *c.*1850. *The extensive contents of his private museum were acquired by the British Museum in 1856*

The "Museum of C. Roach Smith Esq."
F.A.S. Secretary of the Archaeological Association

121
Parts of the late 1st to early 2nd-century *basilica* as recorded by Henry Hodge. *An architect, he recorded for posterity elements of Roman London*

by an architect, Henry Hodge, in advance of destruction. Hodge was also responsible for the careful planning and execution of scale drawings (which still survive) of a large part of the great *basilica* of *c.* AD 100, when the Roman foundations were exposed during construction work for the building of Leadenhall Market in 1881.

Discovery continued to add to the expanding picture of Roman London during the first half of the 20th century, but our knowledge of the layout and composition of the Roman city made dramatic advances when the many rebuilding programmes in the City after the Second World War were preceded by archaeological investigations directed by Professor W F Grimes. Amongst other discoveries these resulted in the identification of the fort in the north-west corner of the City, and the spectacular finding of the Temple of Mithras and its cache of marble sculptures.

The rate of commercial redevelopment and building in the modern City over the last 20 years has ensured the need for both amateur help, and professional archaeological teams both within the City and in Greater London. The next 20 years of rebuilding is likely to lead to the total destruction of the City's archaeology. Reconciling progress with preservation is difficult but the remnants of the Roman city were a determining factor in the City's subsequent growth and surviving remains today now form an important part of its heritage.

ROMAN LONDON TODAY

BOOK LIST

Visible remains of the Roman and later City wall:

1 Corner of City wall; with medieval bastion. GPO Yard. *By prior written arrangement; the Postmaster Controller, King Edward Buildings, King Edward Street, London* EC1A 1AA

2 Line of City wall; with foundations of corner turret and intermediate turret of Roman fort. Noble Street

3 Line of City wall; with post-Roman rebuilding and bastions. In gardens on east side of Museum of London

4 City wall, with Roman (fort) wall at base; above medieval rebuilding and bastions. South of St Giles Cripplegate churchyard

5 City wall, with re-faced Roman (fort) wall and later Roman thickening at base; medieval stone and 15th-century brickwork above. St Alphage churchyard

6 Roman wall. Preserved in east end of underground carpark, London Wall. *Closed at weekends*

7 City wall. Forms the north boundary of churchyard of Church of All Hallows on the Wall

8 Cross-section of Roman wall; with associated earth bank and medieval postern gate. Represented in modern tiling in subway under Houndsditch (Aldgate end), near Irongate House.

9 City wall and base of Roman bastion. Street level viewing platform in car-park at Emperor House, Vine Street. *Open Monday to Friday 8.00 to 18.00; other times or for a closer inspection of the remains by prior written arrangement; the Secretary, Lloyd's Register of Shipping, 71 Fenchurch Street, London* EC3M 4BS

10 City wall, with Roman wall below; early medieval above. Courtyard of 8–10 Cooper's Row

11 City wall and base of Roman internal turret. In gardens directly south of Tower Hill underground

12 City wall and base of Roman bastion. Tower of London

13 Roman riverside wall. Tower of London

Museum of London
London Wall, London EC2Y 5HN
The Roman Gallery records the history of Roman London and displays many of the objects illustrated.
Open: Tuesday to Saturday 10.00 to 18.00; Sunday 14.00 to 18.00

West gate of Roman fort
London Wall
The remains of the northern guard house and gateway of the west gate of the fort, with a section of fort and later defensive wall.
Open: two half days in every month – the 1st Tuesday 10.30 to 12.00; the 3rd Friday 14.30 to 16.00. Visits to the fort gate can be made at other times by school parties and adult groups on application to the Education Officer, Museum of London

British Museum
Great Russell Street, London WC1B 3DG
Displays Roman objects from London, Britain and other parts of the Roman Empire.
Open: Monday to Saturday 10.00 to 17.00; Sunday 14.30 to 18.00

Ground plan of Temple of Mithras
Temple Court,
11 Queen Victoria Street.
Moved and reconstructed from original building material.

The London Wall Walk
Follows the original line of the City Wall for much of its length, from the Tower of London to the Museum of London. The Walk is 1¾ miles (2.8km) long and is marked by panels which can be followed in either direction. Completion of the Walk will take between one and two hours. The information displayed on the panels is reproduced in *The London Wall Walk* booklet, published by the Museum of London.

Books about Roman London

Ralph Merrifield, *London City of the Romans*, Batsford, London (1983): a thorough authoritative account of Roman London and environs, updating the previous books by the same author.

Peter Marsden, *Roman London*, Thames and Hudson, London (1980): an up-to-date account by an archaeologist who writes from first-hand experience, with a useful section on the history of the study of Roman London.

Gustav Milne, *The Port of Roman London*, Batsford, London (1985): a survey of the excavated sections of the Roman waterfront and a detailed discussion of the port and its commercial activities

Regular publications

The London Archaeologist: a magazine of articles by and for London archaeologists, published quarterly since 1968 containing preliminary accounts and discussions on many recent finds.

Transactions and Special Paper series of London & Middlesex Archaeological Society: journals containing detailed reports on recent excavations of Roman sites in the London area, available from the Museum of London bookshop.

General reading

S S Frere, *Britannia: A History of Roman Britain*, Routledge & Kegan Paul, London (1978).

Joan Liversidge, *Britain in the Roman Empire*, Routledge & Kegan Paul, London (1968).

T W Potter, *Roman Britain*, British Museum, London (1983).

Peter Salway, *Roman Britain*, Clarendon Press, Oxford (1981).

John Wacher, *Roman Britain*, Dent, London (1978).